Amazon Associates Blueprint: Building a Lucrative Online Business with Affiliate Marketing

Chase Richardson

Published by CiJiRO Publishing, 2023.

While every precaution has been taken in the preparation of this book, the publisher assumes no responsibility for errors or omissions, or for damages resulting from the use of the information contained herein.

AMAZON ASSOCIATES BLUEPRINT: BUILDING A LUCRATIVE ONLINE BUSINESS WITH AFFILIATE MARKETING

First edition. June 23, 2023.

ISBN: 979-8223350620

Written by Chase Richardson.

Table of Contents

Introduction: 1

Chapter 1: Getting Started with Amazon Associates 4

Chapter 2: Niche Selection and Market Research: Key Components of Amazon Associate Success 12

Chapter 3: Step-by-Step Guide on Building an Affiliate Marketing Website for Amazon Associates 23

Chapter 4: High-Converting Content Creation 42

Chapter 5: Expert Conversion Tips 56

Chapter 6: Scaling Your Affiliate Business with Amazon Associates Program 71

Chapter 7 Key Strategies for Maintaining Your Amazon Affiliate Business 84

Chapter 8: Conclusion 100

Introduction:

Welcome to Amazon Associates Blueprint: Building a Lucrative Online Business with Affiliate Marketing.

In this book, we will explore the exciting world of affiliate marketing and how you can leverage the power of Amazon Associates to create a profitable online business. Whether you are a seasoned marketer or a beginner looking to dive into the world of affiliate marketing, this blueprint will provide you with the knowledge, strategies, and tools you need to succeed.

Affiliate marketing has emerged as one of the most popular and effective ways to monetize online content. It allows individuals to earn commissions by promoting products and services from other companies. Amazon Associates, Amazon's affiliate marketing program, is particularly renowned for its vast product selection, competitive commissions, and trusted brand reputation. By becoming an Amazon Associate, you gain access to a massive marketplace with millions of potential customers, making it an ideal platform to build a lucrative online business.

In this book, we will guide you through the step-by-step process of building a successful Amazon Associates business. We will start by laying the foundation in Chapter 1, where we'll cover the basics of Amazon Associates, how it works, and why it's a great opportunity for aspiring online entrepreneurs.

You will gain a clear understanding of the program's structure, commission rates, and the benefits it offers to both affiliates and customers.

Chapter 2 will delve into the crucial aspect of niche selection and market research. We'll explore various strategies to identify profitable niches that align with your interests and expertise. You'll learn how to evaluate market demand, competition, and profitability to ensure you choose a niche that presents ample opportunities for success.

Once you have identified your niche, Chapter 3 will guide you through the process of building a website or blog to establish your online presence. We'll discuss domain selection, hosting options, and the essential elements of a successful affiliate marketing website. You'll also discover tips for creating a visually appealing and user-friendly platform that engages your target audience.

In Chapter 4, we'll shift our focus to creating high-converting content. Compelling content is the backbone of any successful affiliate marketing strategy. You'll learn how to craft engaging product reviews, informative articles, and other forms of content that not only educate your audience but also entice them to make a purchase through your affiliate links.

Search Engine Optimization (SEO) plays a crucial role in driving organic traffic to your affiliate website, and Chapter 5 will provide you with the tools and techniques to optimize your content for search engines. From keyword research to on-page optimization, we'll cover the essential

SEO practices that will improve your website's visibility and increase your chances of ranking higher in search engine results.

Driving targeted traffic to your website is essential for affiliate marketing success, and Chapter 6 will explore various strategies to accomplish this. You'll learn about social media marketing, email marketing, paid advertising, and other effective methods to attract visitors and convert them into customers.

Chapter 7 will focus on maximizing conversions and earnings. We'll discuss proven strategies to optimize your affiliate links, improve click-through rates, and increase your overall conversion rate. You'll discover the power of split testing, persuasive copywriting techniques, and effective call-to-actions to boost your revenue.

Lastly, in Chapter 8, we'll discuss scaling and growing your Amazon Associates business. We'll explore advanced tactics to expand your reach, diversify your income streams, and leverage automation and outsourcing to free up your time while increasing your profits.

By the end of this book, you'll have a comprehensive understanding of how to build a lucrative online business with affiliate marketing using the Amazon Associates program. You'll be equipped with the knowledge, strategies, and tools necessary to create engaging content, drive targeted traffic, optimize conversions, and scale your business for long-term success. So let's dive in and embark on this exciting journey together!

Chapter 1: Getting Started with Amazon Associates

Welcome to Chapter 1 of Getting Started with Amazon Associates! This blog post will give you a brief introduction to the Amazon Associates program, helping you to understand what it is, how it works, and how you can get started. By the end of this chapter, you'll have a better understanding of what Amazon Associates is all about and how it can help you earn money online. So let's get started!

What is Amazon Associates?

Amazon Associates is a program offered by Amazon that allows individuals to earn money by promoting Amazon products on their website or social media platforms. Essentially, when someone clicks on an affiliate link and makes a purchase through Amazon, the affiliate (or associate) earns a commission on that sale. It's a simple way for website owners or social media influencers to earn a passive income by recommending products they already use and enjoy. Amazon Associates is open to anyone who has a website, blog, YouTube channel, or social media presence, and it's completely free to join. Overall, Amazon Associates is an excellent way to monetize your content and turn your recommendations into a source of income.

Why Become an Amazon Associate?

If you're a blogger, influencer, or website owner, becoming an Amazon Associate can be a lucrative way to earn passive income. Here are a few reasons why you should consider becoming an Amazon Associate:

1. Easy to Use: Amazon Associates is easy to join and easy to use. With just a few clicks, you can become an Amazon

Associate and start earning money from your website.

2. Trusted Brand: Amazon is a trusted brand, which means customers are more likely to buy products through your affiliate links.

3. Commission Structure: Amazon's commission structure is competitive, which means you can earn a significant amount of money with just a few product sales.

4. Product Selection: Amazon offers a wide selection of products to promote, which means you can choose products that align with your niche and audience.

5. Passive Income: Once you promote a product and someone clicks on your affiliate link, you earn a commission on anything they purchase on Amazon within 24 hours. This means you can earn passive income while you sleep!

Overall, becoming an Amazon Associate is an excellent way to monetize your website and earn passive income. Whether you're a blogger, influencer, or website owner, there are many reasons why you should consider becoming an Amazon Associate.

How to Join Amazon Associates

Joining Amazon Associates is a fairly easy process. In fact, it only takes a few minutes to get started.

First, visit the Amazon Associates homepage. Then, click on the "Join Now for Free" button to start the registration process.

You will then be prompted to sign in with your Amazon account or create a new one if you don't already have one. Once you've logged in, you'll need to provide some basic information about yourself, your website or blog, and the types of products you want to promote.

You'll also need to provide your payment and tax information so Amazon can pay you your commission and comply with tax regulations.

After you've provided all the necessary information, you'll be asked to read and agree to the Amazon Associates Operating Agreement, which outlines the terms and conditions of the program.

Once you've completed the registration process and been approved, you'll have access to your Amazon Associates dashboard, where you can start finding products to promote and creating affiliate links to earn commissions.

Overall, joining Amazon Associates is a simple process that can provide you with a great opportunity to earn passive income through affiliate marketing.

Setting Up Your Amazon Associates Account

Now that you've signed up for Amazon Associates, it's time to set up your account. The first step is to fill out your profile information.

Amazon Associates will ask for basic information like your name, address, and tax information. You will also need to provide your website URL(s) where you plan to promote Amazon products.

After you've filled out your profile information, you will need to verify your identity. This involves providing a valid phone number and answering some security questions.

Next, you will need to select your preferred payment method. Amazon offers a variety of payment options, including direct deposit, check, and gift card. Choose the option that works best for you.

Once you've completed these steps, you will be directed to your Amazon Associates dashboard. This is where you will manage your account, find product links, and track your performance and earnings.

Before you can start promoting Amazon products, you will need to create affiliate links. We'll cover how to do that in the next section.

Navigating the Amazon Associates Dashboard

Once you've successfully joined Amazon Associates, you'll be taken to your dashboard. This is where you'll find all the important information you need to manage your account and track your earnings.

The dashboard is split into several sections. The main sections are Home, Reports, Links & Tools, and Settings. Let's take a closer look at each section.

- Home: The Home tab is where you'll find a quick overview of your earnings for the day, month, and year. You'll also see your performance dashboard, which provides an overview of clicks, orders, and earnings for your account.

- Reports: The Reports tab is where you'll find detailed reports on your earnings. You can see your earnings by date range, product category, and more. You can also see how many clicks you're getting and how many of those clicks are converting into sales.

- Links & Tools: The Links & Tools tab is where you'll find all the tools you need to create and manage your affiliate links. You can create links to individual products or create banners and widgets to display on your website. You can also use this section to generate product links for specific countries and to track your link performance.

- Settings: The Settings tab is where you'll find all your account information. You can update your payment settings, add new websites, and manage your user profile.

Overall, the Amazon Associates dashboard is user-friendly and easy to navigate. Take some time to explore the different sections and familiarize yourself with the different features available. By doing so, you'll be able to make the most of your affiliate account and earn more commissions.

Understanding Amazon's Commission Structure

As an Amazon Associate, you will earn a commission for any qualifying purchases made by customers who click on your affiliate links. Amazon's commission structure can vary depending on the product category, but it typically ranges from 1% to 10% of the sale price.

To give you a better idea, let's take a look at some examples. If you promote a book that sells for $20 and has a 4% commission rate, you will earn $0.80 for each sale made through your affiliate link. If you promote a kitchen appliance that sells for $200 and has a 6% commission rate, you will earn $12 for each sale made through your affiliate link.

It's important to note that Amazon's commission structure can change over time and may vary by country or region. Additionally, certain products may not be eligible for commission, such as digital products like ebooks or streaming services.

To stay up-to-date with Amazon's commission rates and policies, make sure to regularly check the Amazon Associates Program Operating Agreement and keep an eye out for any notifications or updates from Amazon.

Understanding Amazon's commission structure is crucial for maximizing your earnings as an Amazon Associate. By focusing on promoting products with higher commission rates and regularly checking for changes to Amazon's policies, you can ensure that you're making the most out of your affiliate marketing efforts.

Benefits of Joining Amazon Associates

Joining the Amazon Associates program offers several benefits for aspiring online entrepreneurs:

Vast Product Selection

One of the significant advantages of Amazon Associates is the extensive range of products available for promotion. Amazon offers millions of items across various categories, ensuring that you can find relevant products for your niche and cater to the diverse needs and interests of your audience.

Trusted Brand Reputation

Amazon is a globally recognized brand known for its exceptional customer service and reliability. Associating yourself with such a reputable brand enhances your credibility as an affiliate marketer. When your audience sees that you are promoting products from

Amazon, they are more likely to trust your recommendations and make a purchase.

Competitive Commission Rates

Amazon offers competitive commission rates, which can range from 1% to 10% or more, depending on the product category. While the commission rates may seem low compared to other affiliate programs, the high conversion rates on Amazon and the sheer volume of potential customers make it a lucrative opportunity.

Cross-Device Conversions

Amazon Associates utilizes cross-device tracking, which means that if a user clicks on your affiliate link on their mobile device but completes the purchase on their desktop later, you still receive the commission. This feature increases your earning potential by capturing conversions that occur across different devices.

Additional Earnings from Upsells

When a customer clicks on your affiliate link and adds other items to their cart before making a purchase, you earn a commission on the entire cart value, not just the promoted product. This "upsell" potential can significantly boost your earnings, especially for higher-priced items.

24/7 Affiliate Support

Amazon provides dedicated affiliate support to help you with any questions or issues you may encounter along the way. Their support team is available 24/7, ensuring that you receive timely assistance whenever you need it.

Now that you understand the basics of Amazon Associates and its benefits, it's time to dive deeper into niche selection and market research in Chapter 2. Identifying a profitable niche is a crucial step toward building a successful affiliate marketing business. So let's move forward and explore how to find the perfect niche for your Amazon Associates venture!

Chapter 2: Niche Selection and Market Research: Key Components of Amazon Associate Success

Niche selection and market research are two of the most important components of success when it comes to becoming an Amazon Associate. Without proper market research and niche selection, it can be difficult to identify the right products to promote and earn commissions from. In this chapter, we'll discuss why niche selection and market research are so important, how to go about selecting the right niche for your Amazon Associate business, and how to conduct effective market research. If you're serious about becoming a successful Amazon Associate, then this chapter is a must-read.

Understanding Niche Selection

When it comes to succeeding as an Amazon Associate, one of the most critical factors is choosing the right niche. Your niche is essentially the specific audience or market you are targeting with your affiliate marketing efforts. Choosing a niche can be a daunting task, but it's crucial to get it right if you want to maximize your earnings.

The first step in understanding niche selection is to recognize the importance of finding a profitable and sustainable niche. If you choose a niche that's too broad or too narrow, you may struggle to attract a dedicated audience. Conversely, if you choose a niche that's too competitive, you'll find it challenging to make your mark.

To avoid these pitfalls, consider your interests, passions, and areas of expertise. Do you have any specialized knowledge or skills that could help you succeed in a particular niche? Is there an audience that you feel particularly drawn to, and that you could serve well with your content?

Once you've identified potential niches, it's important to evaluate their profitability. Look for niches that have a large and dedicated audience, with products and services that offer high commission rates. It's also important to consider the potential for growth and sustainability. Will this niche still be viable in five years? Ten years?

Ultimately, understanding niche selection is all about finding the sweet spot between a market with a high potential for profit and one that aligns with your passions and interests. With a solid niche in place, you'll be better equipped to build a loyal audience and achieve success as an Amazon Associate.

The Importance of Market Research

Before you dive headfirst into any new business venture, it's essential to conduct thorough market research. As an Amazon Associate, your success largely depends on the niche you select and the products you promote within that niche. Without proper market research, you risk investing your time and effort in a niche that won't generate enough profit to sustain your business.

Market research involves analyzing market trends, understanding your target audience, and identifying potential competitors. By doing so, you'll gain insight into what products your target audience is searching for, what their pain points are, and how you can meet their needs with Amazon products.

Here are some key components of market research to consider:

- **Analyze market trends**: What are the latest trends in your niche? What products are currently popular, and why?

- **Understand your target audience:** Who is your target audience? What are their pain points, demographics, and interests?

- **Identify potential competitors:** Who else is selling products in your niche? What products are they selling, and how are they marketing them?

- **Look for gaps in the market:** Are there any products or services that are currently missing in your niche? Is there an opportunity for you to fill that gap?

- **Consider market demand:** Is there a high demand for products in your niche? Are people actively searching for these products online?

By conducting thorough market research, you'll be better equipped to select a profitable niche and choose products that will resonate with your target audience. You'll also have a better understanding of your competition and how you can differentiate yourself from them. Don't rush this crucial step - take the time to research and analyze your niche before you start promoting products as an Amazon Associate.

Identifying Profitable Niches

Once you've decided to become an Amazon Associate, one of the first things you need to do is to identify profitable niches that you can focus on. A niche is a specific area of interest, such as a particular product, industry, or subject matter, that you can specialize in and build a website or blog around.

To identify profitable niches, you need to consider a few different factors. First, you want to look for niches that have high demand. You can use tools like Google Trends or the Google Keyword Planner to research the popularity of different niches and see which ones are trending up or down.

Second, you want to look for niches that have low competition. If there are already hundreds or thousands of other websites or blogs in your chosen niche, it will be very difficult to rank highly in search engines and attract traffic to your site.

Third, you want to look for niches that have a high-profit margin. Some niches, such as luxury items or high-end electronics, may offer larger commissions than others.

Finally, you want to consider your own interests and expertise. It's much easier to create content and promote products that you're passionate about or have experience with.

To get started, brainstorm a list of potential niches that meet these criteria. Then, use tools like the Amazon Best Sellers list or niche-specific forums and social media groups to research potential products and services to promote. Remember to also consider the level of investment required to establish your niche as well as its sustainability. With these factors in mind, you'll be on your way to identifying a profitable niche for your Amazon Associate business.

Analyzing Competition

When it comes to niche selection and market research for the Amazon Associate program, analyzing competition is crucial. This step involves examining other websites, blogs, and Amazon product listings that are targeting your chosen niche. By analyzing your competition, you'll be able to understand their strengths and weaknesses, as well as gain insights into what is working in the niche.

Start by doing a Google search for your niche keywords and examining the top-ranked websites that show up in the search results. Look for patterns in the content they publish, the products they promote, and the audience they target. Take notes on what you like and what you don't like about their approach. Google Trends is also a great free tool to see interest in topics and products over different periods of time and geographic locations you are targeting.

Next, use Amazon to examine the competition on a more granular level. Look at the top-selling products in your niche and take note of their prices, features, and customer reviews. Identify any gaps or opportunities where you could create a better product offering, fill a void, or provide more value to customers.

One thing to keep in mind is that not all competition is bad. In fact, seeing other successful websites and products in your niche can indicate a healthy and thriving market. You want to find a balance between a niche that is too competitive and one that is too niche to generate substantial revenue.

Finally, make sure to check out the competition on social media as well. See how they are engaging with their audience, what type of content they are sharing, and what their social media strategy is. This information can give you insights into what type of content performs well in the niche and how you can tailor your content to better connect with your audience.

Overall, analyzing competition is a vital step in the niche selection and market research process for the Amazon Associate program. By understanding your competition, you'll be able to identify gaps in the market, craft a better value proposition, and ultimately stand out in a crowded field.

Conducting Keyword Research

Once you've identified your niche and have a general idea of what your target audience is searching for, it's time to conduct keyword research. This process involves finding the keywords and phrases that people are using to search for products or information related to your niche.

There are many tools available to help you conduct keyword research, but one of the most popular is Google's Keyword Planner. This tool allows you to enter a keyword or phrase related to your niche and see how many searches it receives each month, as well as how competitive it is to rank for that keyword.

Other tools like *SEMrush*, *Ahrefs*, and *Moz* also offer keyword research features that can help you identify long-tail keywords (phrases with three or more words) that may be easier to rank for and that are highly relevant to your niche.

Once you've identified your target keywords, you can begin optimizing your content around them. This includes using the keywords in your page titles, headings, and throughout your content in a natural way that doesn't feel forced.

Remember, while it's important to use keywords in your content, it's equally important to focus on providing high-quality, informative content that your readers will find valuable. Keyword stuffing or over-optimizing your content can actually hurt your search rankings and turn off your readers.

By conducting thorough keyword research and optimizing your content around your target keywords, you'll be better positioned to attract traffic to your Amazon Associate website and increase your chances of earning commissions on the products you promote.

Testing Your Niche Ideas

After conducting extensive research on potential niches and identifying ones with high-profit potential, it's time to put your ideas to the test. This process will allow you to determine which niches are worth pursuing and which ones may not be worth the time and effort.

One effective way to test your niche ideas is by creating a website or blog focused on your chosen niche. This will allow you to produce content and build an audience while monitoring traffic and engagement levels. It's important to track your website's analytics to see if your niche is attracting traffic and if your audience is engaged with your content.

Another approach is to test different affiliate products within your niche. By promoting a variety of products, you'll be able to see which ones resonate with your audience and result in higher sales commissions. It's important to keep track of your sales data to determine which products are worth promoting long-term.

Additionally, seeking feedback from your audience through surveys or social media can provide valuable insights into their interests and preferences. This information can help you fine-tune your niche and promotional strategy to better cater to your audience's needs.

Ultimately, testing your niche ideas is a crucial step in the Amazon Associate program journey. It will help you determine the viability and profitability of your chosen niche, allowing you to focus your efforts on areas that have the greatest potential for success.

Profitability and Commission Potential

As an Amazon Associate, your primary goal is to make money through affiliate commissions. That's why it's essential to consider the profitability and commission potential of your chosen niche.

The first thing you need to consider is the price range of the products in your niche. It's much easier to earn a decent commission from higher-priced products than lower-priced ones. For instance, if you promote a product worth $500 with a 5% commission, you'll earn $25 per sale. But, if you promote a $50 product with the same commission, you'll only earn $2.5 per sale.

You should also take into account the average conversion rate of the products in your niche. This conversion rate shows the percentage of visitors to your website who make a purchase. It's crucial to choose products with a high conversion rate since it means that more of your visitors are likely to make a purchase.

Another important factor to consider is the commission rate offered by Amazon. Generally, Amazon offers a commission rate of between 4% and 10%, depending on the category. You need to choose a niche that has a high commission rate to increase your earning potential.

In addition to these factors, you should also consider the demand for the products in your niche. The higher the demand, the more likely you are to earn commissions.

To ensure that you're making a profitable decision, it's crucial to conduct a thorough analysis of your niche and its potential for commission earnings. Keep track of your earnings over time, and regularly evaluate your performance to identify any opportunities for improvement.

By carefully considering the profitability and commission potential of your niche, you can increase your chances of success as an Amazon Associate.

Longevity and Growth Potential

When it comes to niche selection and market research for the Amazon Associate program, it's essential to consider both the short-term and long-term potential of your chosen niche. While a niche might seem profitable in the short-term, it might not have the potential to grow and sustain over time. Therefore, you need to think strategically about the future growth of your niche.

To identify the longevity and growth potential of your chosen niche, start by researching the market trends, consumer demand, and competition. Determine whether there is a growing demand for the products or services within your niche and whether it has the potential to become a long-term trend. Also, research the market saturation within your niche to see how many competitors are already present.

Once you've identified the potential of your niche, it's crucial to think about how you can grow it over time. Consider whether there are any opportunities for diversification or expansion within your niche. Can you offer complementary products or services to your target audience, or can you expand your reach by targeting new sub-niches within your broader niche?

Furthermore, think about how you can leverage technology and digital marketing strategies to grow your niche over time. Can you create engaging content, optimize your website for search engines, or tap into social media to attract more traffic and customers?

Ultimately, your goal should be to create a niche that has both short-term profitability and long-term growth potential. By identifying the right niche and implementing effective growth strategies, you can achieve success as an Amazon Associate and build a sustainable income stream over time.

Chapter 3: Step-by-Step Guide on Building an Affiliate Marketing Website for Amazon Associates

Are you looking to build an affiliate marketing website for the Amazon Associates program? It can be overwhelming at first, but don't worry! This chapter will take you through the process of building a successful website or blog that can generate income through the Amazon Associates program. In this guide, you'll learn how to choose a domain name, create content, choose the right hosting service, and more. Let's get started!

Understanding the Importance of a Website for Affiliate Marketing

If you're looking to build a successful affiliate marketing business, then creating a website or blog is absolutely essential. Not only will it help establish your brand and credibility in your chosen niche, but it will also serve as a platform for promoting your affiliate links and generating revenue through Amazon Associates.

Without a website, you're essentially limiting yourself to just promoting products through social media, which can be incredibly challenging and not very effective. With a website, however, you can create targeted content that speaks directly to your audience and helps guide them toward making a purchase.

Another benefit of having a website is that it allows you to capture leads and build an email list, which is critical for building a long-term affiliate marketing strategy. With an email list, you can continue to engage with your audience and promote products even after they've left your site, which can result in more sales and revenue over time.

In short, a website is absolutely essential for building a successful affiliate marketing business with Amazon Associates. It's not only a platform for promoting products, but it also helps establish your brand, build credibility, capture leads, and engage with your audience over the long term. So if you haven't already, it's time to start thinking about building your own website or blog to help take your affiliate marketing game to the next level.

Choosing a Niche for Your Website

One of the first things you need to do when building a website for affiliate marketing is choosing a niche. Your niche is the topic or subject area that your website will focus on. Choosing a niche is essential for two reasons: it will help you build an audience and attract the right kind of traffic, and it will help you choose the right products to promote on your site.

To choose a niche, start by thinking about your interests and expertise. Ideally, you should choose a topic that you are passionate about and have some knowledge of. This will make it easier for you to create high-quality content and engage with your audience.

Next, consider the profitability of your niche. While it's important to choose a topic that you enjoy, you also need to make sure that it has the potential to generate revenue. Look for niches that have a significant market size and demand, and that offer products or services with a high commission rate.

When choosing a niche for Amazon Associates, it's also important to consider the types of products that are available on the platform. Take some time to research the different product categories on Amazon, and look for products that align with your niche and have good reviews.

Once you've chosen your niche, make sure that you can create enough content to keep your website fresh and engaging. You should aim to create a range of content types, including blog posts, product reviews, how-to guides, and more.

Overall, choosing the right niche is a crucial step in building a successful affiliate marketing website. By selecting a topic that you're passionate about and that has good earning potential, you'll be setting yourself up for success and helping your website stand out from the competition.

Setting Up Your Domain Name and Hosting

Once you have decided on your niche and your website's CMS, it is time to set up your domain name and hosting. This is the first step in creating a website, as it will allow you to create a space online that people can visit and engage with your content.

A domain name is your website's address on the internet, and it needs to be unique and memorable. You can purchase a domain name through a registrar such as GoDaddy, Namecheap, or HostGator. The cost of a domain name can vary, but it typically ranges from $10 to $20 per year. When choosing a domain name, try to pick something that reflects your niche and is easy to remember.

Hosting is the space where your website's files and data will be stored, and it allows your website to be accessible to visitors online. There are several web hosting providers to choose from, including Bluehost, HostGator, and SiteGround. The cost of hosting can vary, but it typically ranges from $2.95 to $5.95 per month, depending on the provider and plan you choose. If you want easy to setup and dedicated Wordpress hosting, I highly recommend Hostinger as an easy to setup, all in one solution, at a very reasonable cost.

When selecting a hosting provider, it is important to consider factors such as uptime, customer support, and server location. A good hosting provider will have reliable uptime, 24/7 customer support, and servers that are located close to your target audience to ensure fast load times.

After you have selected a domain name and hosting provider, you will need to connect your domain name to your hosting account. This can usually be done through your hosting provider's control panel or by updating your domain name's DNS settings. Once this is complete, you can install WordPress and start building your website.

Remember, your domain name and hosting provider are essential to the success of your website, so take the time to choose a reliable provider and a memorable domain name. With the right tools and resources, you can create a professional website that drives traffic and conversions for your Amazon Associates program.

Choosing a Content Management System (CMS)

Once you have registered your domain name and hosting, the next step in building your affiliate marketing website is choosing a content management system (CMS). A CMS is an application that allows you to create, edit, and manage digital content. It makes building and updating your website easier and faster, even if you don't have advanced technical skills.

There are a few different CMS options out there, including WordPress, Joomla, Drupal, and others. However, WordPress is by far the most popular and widely used CMS, and for good reason. It is free, user-friendly, customizable, and SEO-friendly.

When selecting a CMS, consider the following factors:

1. Ease of Use: The CMS should be user-friendly, even for those with limited technical knowledge.

2. Customizability: The CMS should be easily customizable, allowing you to change the appearance and functionality of your website.

3. SEO-Friendliness: The CMS should be optimized for search engines, ensuring your website can rank higher on Google.

4. Security: The CMS should be secure, protecting your website and its visitors from potential threats.

Once you have weighed these factors, it is likely that WordPress will be your top choice for building an affiliate marketing website.

In the next section, we will guide you through installing WordPress and choosing a theme for your website.

Installing WordPress and Choosing a Theme

Once you have set up your domain name and hosting, it's time to install a content management system (CMS). WordPress is the most popular CMS platform, and it's easy to use, even if you're not tech-savvy. Here's how to install WordPress on your site:

1. Log in to your hosting account's control panel.

2. Look for the WordPress installer, usually found in the "Software" or "Apps" section.

3. Follow the installer's instructions, choosing your domain name and entering a username and password.

4. Once the installation is complete, log in to your WordPress dashboard.

Congratulations, you now have a website that's powered by WordPress!

Now, it's time to choose a theme. A theme is a template that creates how your website looks and feels. It's important to choose a theme that suits your niche and brand. Here are some tips for selecting a theme:

1. Choose a responsive theme: A responsive theme adapts to different screen sizes, which is crucial because more and more people are browsing the web on mobile devices.

2. Look for a theme with clean design: Avoid cluttered or complicated themes. A clean, simple design is best for usability and conversion.

3. Check the customization options: Make sure the theme allows you to customize colors, fonts, and other design elements easily.

4. Read reviews and check ratings: Look for a theme with good ratings and positive reviews from other users.

5. Choose a theme that's compatible with your plugins: Make sure the theme is compatible with any plugins you plan to use on your site.

Once you've chosen a theme, it's time to install and activate it in your WordPress dashboard. Go to Appearance > Themes > Add New and search for your chosen theme. Click "Install" and then "Activate" once it's installed.

With WordPress and your chosen theme installed, you now have a fully functioning website. In the next section, we'll discuss how to configure WordPress settings for SEO.

Configuring WordPress Settings for SEO

Search Engine Optimization (SEO) is crucial when it comes to building a successful website for affiliate marketing. By optimizing your website's SEO, you can increase your chances of ranking higher on search engine results pages, which ultimately drives more traffic to your site.

To configure your WordPress settings for SEO, follow these steps:

1. Install an SEO Plugin: There are several SEO plugins available for WordPress, such as Yoast SEO or All in One SEO Pack. Choose one that fits your needs and install it.

2. Configure General Settings: Once your SEO plugin is installed, navigate to the settings page. Here, you can configure the general settings, such as your site's title and meta description. This information will appear in search engine results pages, so make sure it accurately reflects your website's content.

3. Set Permalinks: Permalinks are the URLs of your website's pages and posts. They should be easy to read and contain relevant keywords. Go to Settings > Permalinks and choose a structure that makes sense for your website.

4. Enable XML Sitemap: An XML sitemap helps search engines crawl your website and understand its structure. Your SEO plugin should automatically generate an XML sitemap for you. Check the settings to ensure it's enabled and up-to-date.

5. Add Schema Markup: Schema markup is a type of code that provides more information to search engines about your website's content. It can help improve your website's visibility in search results. There are several WordPress plugins available that make it easy to add schema markup to your site.

6. Optimize Your Content: Finally, make sure all of your website's content is optimized for SEO. This means using relevant keywords, creating high-quality content, and including internal and external links.

Your SEO plugin should provide suggestions and tips for optimizing your content.

By configuring your WordPress settings for SEO, you can improve your website's visibility in search engine results pages and drive more traffic to your site. Remember to regularly monitor your website's analytics and make adjustments as necessary to continually improve your SEO efforts.

Adding Essential Pages to Your Website

Once you have your domain name, hosting, and content management system in place, it's time to start adding essential pages to your website. These pages not only provide necessary information for your audience, but they also improve the user experience and help your site rank higher in search engines.

1. About Page

Your website's "About" page is where you introduce yourself and your business to your audience. This is where you can showcase your expertise and explain what makes your site unique. Be sure to include a clear call-to-action and ways for readers to connect with you.

2. Contact Page

The "Contact" page is where visitors can get in touch with you directly. This page should include a form or email address for visitors to use to contact you. You can also include your social media handles, phone number, or other contact information here.

3. Privacy Policy

Your website must have a privacy policy in place to inform visitors about how their data is collected, used, and protected. This page is especially important if you plan on collecting any personal information from visitors through forms or cookies.

4. Terms and Conditions

Your "Terms and Conditions" page outlines the rules and guidelines for using your site. This can include information about your affiliate partnerships, a disclaimer of liability, copyright information, and more.

If you're planning on using a blog to create content for your affiliate site, this page is where you'll showcase all your posts. Your blog can be a powerful tool for driving traffic to your site and building authority in your niche.

5. Product Reviews and Recommendations

Finally, your website should have a dedicated section for product reviews and recommendations. This is where you'll showcase your affiliate products and services and explain why you recommend them. This page is critical to your affiliate marketing strategy, so be sure to invest time and effort into creating high-quality, trustworthy content that converts.

By adding these essential pages to your website, you'll improve the user experience and create a professional, trustworthy online presence. This will help attract more visitors to your site, boost your SEO efforts, and increase your affiliate earnings.

Creating High-Quality Content that Converts

When it comes to building a successful affiliate marketing website for Amazon Associates, creating high-quality content that converts should be one of your top priorities. Your content should not only attract visitors to your site, but also encourage them to take action by clicking on your affiliate links and making a purchase on Amazon.

Here are some guidelines for creating content that converts:

1. Know Your Audience: knowing who your target audience is the key to creating content that resonates with them. Conduct market research to identify their interests, needs, and pain points. Use this information to tailor your content to their specific needs and interests.

2. Focus on Product Reviews: Product reviews are a great way to showcase the benefits and features of the products you are promoting. Write detailed reviews that provide value to your readers and help them make an informed buying decision.

3. Use Engaging Visuals: Visual content is more engaging and memorable than text alone. Use high-quality images, videos, and infographics to break up text and add interest to your content.

4. Optimizing your Content for Search Engines: Use relevant phrases and keywords throughout your content to improve your search engine rankings. This will help more people find your content and increase the likelihood of them clicking on your affiliate links.

5. Be Honest and Transparent: Transparency is key in affiliate marketing. Be honest with your readers about your affiliate relationships and only promote products that you genuinely believe in and have used yourself.

By focusing on creating high-quality content that converts, you can build a loyal following of readers who trust your recommendations and are more likely to make a purchase through your affiliate links.

Building a Social Media Presence to Promote Your Site

Once your affiliate marketing website is up and running, the next step is to build a strong social media presence to drive traffic to your site and increase conversions. Social media can be an incredibly powerful tool for affiliate marketers, as it provides an opportunity to engage with your audience and promote your content in a more organic way.

Here are some tips for building a social media presence to promote your affiliate marketing website:

1. Choose the Right Platforms:

There are dozens of social media platforms out there, but not all of them will be right for your affiliate marketing website. Choose platforms that are popular with your target audience and focus your efforts there. For example, if you're targeting younger consumers, Instagram and Snapchat may be more effective than Facebook or LinkedIn.

2. Create Engaging Content:

Social media is all about engagement, so make sure your content is interesting, informative, and shareable. Share your latest blog posts, reviews, and other content that your audience will find useful and valuable. Consider incorporating visuals like images and videos to make your content stand out.

3. Be Consistent:

Consistency is always key when building a social media presence online. Post regularly and engage with your followers regularly. You don't need to post every day, but you should have a regular posting schedule that your followers can expect.

4. Use Hashtags:

Hashtags are excellent in getting your content in front of a larger audience. Research relevant hashtags in your niche and use them in your posts to increase visibility and reach.

5. Leverage Influencers:

Partnering with influencers in your niche can be a powerful way to reach a larger audience and drive traffic to your site. Look for influencers who have a strong following and are relevant to your niche, and offer to collaborate on content or promotions.

6. Monitor Your Results:

Track your social media metrics to see what's working and what's not. Look for patterns in engagement and clicks to identify what types of content and strategies are resonating with your audience.

By following these tips, you can build a strong social media presence that drives traffic to your affiliate marketing website and increases your conversions. Remember to focus on providing value to your audience and engaging with them regularly, and your social media presence will naturally grow over time.

Implementing Amazon Associates Links into Your Content

Once your website is up and running with high-quality content, it's time to start incorporating Amazon Associates links into your pages. Amazon Associates is a great way to earn commission on products sold through your website.

First, log in to your Amazon Associates account and find the products you want to promote. You can search for specific products, or browse by category or keyword.

Once you've found a product you want to promote, click the "Get link" button to generate your unique affiliate link. This link includes a special tracking code that allows Amazon to credit you with a commission for any sales made through your link.

Now, it's time to incorporate these links into your content. You can add affiliate links to text, images, and buttons on your website. Be sure to disclose that you're using affiliate links, as required by the FTC.

When adding links to your content, focus on products that are relevant to your niche and audience. You want to promote products that your audience will be interested in and likely to purchase. Don't spam your content with links to unrelated products or you risk turning off your audience.

Finally, track your earnings through the Amazon Associates dashboard. This will give you valuable insights into which products are selling well and how much commission you're earning.

Remember, earning money through Amazon Associates takes time and effort. You won't see results overnight, but if you consistently create high-quality content and promote products your audience loves, you can build a successful affiliate marketing website.

Building an Email List

While building a website is important for affiliate marketing, having an email list is just as crucial. This allows you to have a direct line of communication with your audience, and you can promote your affiliate links directly to them.

To start building your email list, you will need an email marketing service provider. There are several options available, but popular ones include Mailchimp, ConvertKit, and Aweber. These providers will allow you to create and manage your email list, as well as send newsletters and other emails to your subscribers.

Once you have signed up for an email marketing service provider, you can start collecting email addresses on your website. You can do this by adding a sign-up form to your website, either in a pop-up or a widget on your homepage or sidebar.

To encourage people to sign up for your email list, offer them something of value in return, such as a free e-book, a discount code, or access to exclusive content. Make sure to highlight the benefits of being on your email list and how it can help them solve a problem or achieve a goal.

As you start to build your email list, it's important to segment your subscribers based on their interests or behaviors. This will allow you to send targeted emails to specific groups, increasing the chances of conversions.

When it comes to promoting your affiliate links via email, make sure to follow best practices and avoid spamming your subscribers. Only promote products that you genuinely believe in and provide value to your audience. Make sure to include clear and prominent disclosures about your affiliate relationship with Amazon in your emails, as required by the Federal Trade Commission.

Building an email list takes time and effort, but it can be a powerful tool for affiliate marketing. By nurturing your list and providing valuable content, you can increase conversions and generate more revenue as an Amazon Associate.

Congratulations! With your website or blog up and running, you are now ready to start creating valuable content, promoting affiliate products, and growing your audience. In the next chapter, we will explore various strategies for driving targeted traffic to your website and maximizing your affiliate marketing conversions.

Chapter 4: High-Converting Content Creation

Are you looking to get the most out of your Amazon Associates affiliate program? Creating content with high conversion rates is key to becoming a top-performing affiliate. chapter, we'll discuss the best tips for crafting effective content to maximize your Amazon Associates' success. We'll cover topics such as keyword research, optimizing visuals, and creating high-quality content. With this information in hand, you'll be well on your way to becoming a top-performing Amazon Associate. So, let's get started!

Understanding the Importance of High-Converting Content

As an Amazon Associates affiliate, creating high-converting content should be at the top of your priority list. Why? Because high-converting content has the power to turn readers into buyers and ultimately increase your commissions.

But what exactly is high-converting content? Essentially, it is content that persuades your readers to take action – whether that be purchasing a product, signing up for a service, or clicking on an affiliate link.

The benefits of high-converting content are clear: more clicks, more sales, and ultimately more commission for you as an affiliate. However, creating high-converting content isn't always easy – it requires time, effort, and skill.

That said, it is important to note that the success of your affiliate marketing efforts largely depends on the quality of your content. Content marketing is one of the most effective ways to drive traffic to your affiliate site and boost conversions.

So, to become a top-performing affiliate, you must understand the importance of high-converting content and make it a priority in your affiliate marketing strategy. By doing so, you can create content that engages and converts your readers into loyal customers, leading to long-term success as an Amazon Associates affiliate.

Choosing Profitable Niches and Products

As an Amazon Associates affiliate, the first step to creating high-converting content is choosing the right niche and products. It's important to choose products that are not only popular and in demand, but also have a high commission rate. A product with a low commission rate may be popular, but it won't bring in the revenue you're looking for.

Start by researching niches that align with your interests and expertise. This will make it easier for you to create content that is not only high-quality but also informative and engaging for your audience. Once you've identified a few niches, start looking for products within those niches that have high demand and high commission rates.

One way to identify profitable products is by checking their Amazon Best Sellers Rank. This will give you an idea of how popular a product is within its category. You can also look at customer reviews to see how satisfied customers are with the product.

Another way to find profitable products is by using Amazon's Product Advertising API. This tool allows you to search for products by keyword, category, and other criteria. You can also see the commission rate for each product and its sales rank.

When choosing products, also consider the type of content you plan to create. For example, if you plan to write product reviews, look for products with a lot of positive reviews and high ratings. If you plan to create video content, consider products that are visually appealing and easy to demonstrate.

Overall, choosing profitable niches and products is crucial to creating high-converting content as an Amazon Associates affiliate. Take the time to do your research and choose products that align with your audience's interests and needs, and that offer a high commission rate. You will be able to create content that not only engages your audience but also generates revenue for your business.

Conducting Effective Keyword Research for SEO

If you want to create high-converting content that attracts visitors and earns you commissions through Amazon Associates, it's crucial to start by conducting effective keyword research for SEO.

Here are a few tips to help you get started:

1. Use Keyword Research Tools: There are many tools available to help you research and identify the best keywords for your content. Some popular options include Google Keyword Planner, Ahrefs, SEMrush, and Moz Keyword Explorer. By using these tools, you can uncover the most relevant and high-traffic keywords to target.

2. Identify Your Target Audience: When conducting keyword research, it's important to keep your target audience in mind. What phrases or search terms are they using to find the types of products you are promoting? This information will help you create content that is both relevant and engaging for your audience.

3. Focus on Long-Tail Keywords: While it's important to target high-traffic keywords, it's also essential to focus on long-tail keywords. These phrases are more specific and targeted, making them easier to rank for and more likely to convert into sales.

4. Analyze Competitor Keywords: Another helpful strategy is to analyze the keywords your competitors are using in their content. This can help you identify gaps in the market and find new opportunities to target.

5. Don't Overdo it: Finally, it's important to remember that keyword stuffing can actually harm your SEO efforts. Be sure to use your keywords naturally throughout your content, and focus on creating valuable, high-quality content that your readers will appreciate.

By conducting effective keyword research, you can ensure that your content is optimized for SEO and more likely to attract the right audience and earn you commissions through the Amazon Associates program.

Crafting Compelling Headlines and Introductions

When it comes to creating high-converting content, your headlines and introductions play a crucial role. They're the first things your readers see, and if they don't capture their attention, you'll lose them before they even start reading.

To craft compelling headlines and introductions, you need to understand your audience and what they're looking for. You should also aim to make your content unique and stand out from the competition.

Here are some tips to help you create attention-grabbing headlines and introductions:

1. Use numbers: People love lists and the numerical nature of a headline is something which would make it more appealing. For example, "10 Ways to Save Money on Amazon" or "5 Must-Have Products for Your Home Office."

2. Make a promise: Tell your readers what they'll get out of your content. For example, "How to Double Your Amazon Affiliate Earnings in 30 Days" or "The Ultimate Guide to Finding Profitable Niches on Amazon."

3. Be descriptive: Use vivid language to paint a picture of what your readers will learn or discover in your content. For example, "Uncover the Secrets to Amazon's Most Successful Affiliates" or "Discover the Hidden Gems of Amazon's Product Marketplace."

4. Ask a question: This can pique your readers' curiosity and make them want to find out the answer. For example, "Can You Really Make a Full-Time Income as an Amazon Affiliate?" or "What Do Top-Performing Amazon Affiliates Know that You Don't?"

5. Use humor: If appropriate for your niche and audience, injecting a bit of humor into your headlines and introductions can make them more memorable and shareable. For example, "Why Amazon's CEO Should Be Worried About Your Affiliate Earnings" or "How to Slay the Amazon Affiliate Game and Still Have Time for Netflix."

Remember, your headlines and introductions are your first chance to make a great impression on your readers. Don't be afraid to get creative and experiment with different approaches until you find what works best for your audience and content.

Writing Reviews that Convert Readers into Buyers

One of the most important aspects of creating high-converting content for Amazon Associates is writing reviews that effectively persuade readers to make a purchase. The following tips will help you craft reviews that convert readers into buyers:

1. Be honest and transparent: Your reviews should provide a balanced assessment of the product, highlighting both its strengths and weaknesses. Being honest and transparent will build trust with your audience and increase the likelihood of them making a purchase through your affiliate link.

2. Focus on benefits: Rather than just listing the features of the product, focus on the benefits that it provides to the user. For example, instead of saying "this vacuum has a powerful motor," you could say "this vacuum will effortlessly suck up dirt and debris, leaving your floors spotless."

3. Use visuals: Including high-quality images and videos of the product can help readers visualize how it will look and function in their own lives. This can increase their desire to purchase the product.

4. Include comparisons: Comparing the product to other similar products on the market can help readers understand how it stands out from the competition. Be sure to highlight the unique benefits of the product that set it apart from its competitors.

5. Address common objections: Addressing common objections that readers may have about the product can help overcome their hesitations. For example, if the product is more expensive than similar products on the market, you could explain why the additional cost is worth it in terms of quality and performance.

6. End with a strong call to action: Your review should end with a strong call to action that encourages readers to make a purchase through your affiliate link. Be sure to emphasize the urgency and importance of taking action now to secure the product before it sells out.

By following these tips, you can craft reviews that effectively convert readers into buyers, maximizing your earnings as an Amazon Associates affiliate.

Incorporating Amazon Associates Links and Widgets into Your Content

Now that you have created high-converting content, it's time to start incorporating Amazon Associates links and widgets into your posts. These links and widgets allow your readers to purchase products directly from Amazon, and as an affiliate, you earn a commission on those sales.

First, let's talk about links. When you are writing a post, think about what products your readers would be interested in. For example, if you are writing a post about the best running shoes, you could include links to the top-rated shoes on Amazon. You can also include links in your reviews to the specific product you are reviewing.

It's important to note that the links you include must be formatted correctly to track your commissions. Amazon provides a tool called SiteStripe that makes it easy to create these links. Simply log in to your Amazon Associates account, navigate to the product page you want to link to, and click on the SiteStripe toolbar at the top of your screen. From there, you can create a text link, image link, or add the product to a carousel widget.

Widgets are another great way to incorporate Amazon Associates links into your content. Widgets allow you to showcase multiple products in a visually appealing way. You can create a widget for a specific category or even for a specific product. Amazon offers several types of widgets, including image and text links, as well as carousels and grids.

When incorporating links and widgets into your content, be sure to keep them relevant and useful for your readers. Don't overload your posts with links or include products that don't fit with the theme of your post. Remember, the goal is to create high-converting content that your readers will appreciate and find valuable.

In addition to links and widgets, you can also promote products on your social media channels. When you share your posts on social media, be sure to include Amazon Associates links so your followers can easily purchase the products you recommend.

In the next section, we will discuss optimizing your content for mobile devices. Stay tuned!

Optimizing Your Content for Mobile Devices

In today's fast-paced world, more and more people are accessing the internet via their mobile devices. This means that it's more important than ever to optimize your content for mobile devices if you want to see success with the Amazon Associates affiliate program.

If you want to maximize your content for mobile devices, these are a few crucial considerations. Firstly, you'll want to ensure that your website is mobile-friendly and responsive. This means that it should be easy to navigate on a small screen and that images and text should be optimized for mobile viewing.

Another important consideration is page speed. Mobile users tend to have shorter attention spans than desktop users, so it's crucial that your content loads quickly. You can improve your page speed by optimizing images and minimizing the use of scripts and plugins.

When it comes to your content itself, you'll want to keep things concise and easy to read on a small screen. This means using shorter paragraphs and subheadings to break up the text, as well as using bullet points and lists where appropriate.

Finally, make sure that any Amazon Associates links or widgets that you use are optimized for mobile as well. Ensure that they are easy to click on a small screen, and that they don't interfere with the overall user experience.

By taking these steps to optimize your content for mobile devices, you'll be able to reach a wider audience and maximize your earnings with the Amazon Associates program. So don't neglect mobile optimization - it's a crucial part of any successful affiliate marketing strategy.

Promoting Your Content on Social Media

You can promote your content through social media in today's digital age. Platforms like Facebook, Twitter, and Instagram allow you to reach a wide audience and drive traffic to your website. However, promoting your content on social media requires a strategic approach.

First and foremost, you need to understand your audience and choose the social media platforms they frequent the most. For example, if your target audience is primarily women, then platforms like Pinterest and Instagram would be more effective than Twitter.

Once you have identified the platforms you want to use, it's time to create a content calendar. Consistency is key when it comes to promoting your content on social media. You should post regularly and at specific times to maximize your reach.

When promoting your content on social media, it's important to use eye-catching visuals and headlines. People are more likely to engage with content that is visually appealing and informative. Use high-quality images and graphics that showcase your products and entice readers to click through to your website.

In addition to posting on your own social media profiles, consider collaborating with influencers and bloggers in your niche. This can help expand your reach and drive more traffic to your website. You can also participate in relevant social media groups and communities where your target audience is active.

Finally, track and analyze your social media performance. Use analytics tools to measure the engagement and conversion rates of your social media posts. This data can help you refine your strategy and improve your content to maximize your ROI.

By promoting your content strategically on social media, you can drive more traffic to your website and increase your chances of earning commissions through the Amazon Associates program.

Measuring and Analyzing the Performance of Your Content

One of the key components of creating high-converting content is measuring and analyzing its performance. Without tracking the effectiveness of your content, you won't be able to understand what is working and what isn't, and therefore you won't be able to improve.

Here are some metrics you should track in order to evaluate your content's success:

1. Traffic: The number of visitors to your site will give you a sense of the overall reach of your content.

2. Engagement: What is the average duration of visits to your site? Are they clicking on links or scrolling through multiple pages?

3. Conversion rate: This metric tells you how many visitors took a desired action, such as making a purchase through one of your affiliate links.

4. Click-through rate: This metric measures the percentage of people who click on your affiliate links after reading your content.

5. Revenue: Finally, track the amount of revenue generated by your content through Amazon Associates.

Once you have collected this data, you can start to analyze what is working and what isn't. Perhaps you'll find that certain types of content are more effective than others, or that certain product categories convert better than others. Use this information to make changes and tweaks to your content strategy and optimize your results.

The best part about measuring and analyzing your content's performance is that you can do it over time. Keep track of the metrics over the long term, and you'll be able to see how your content performs as trends and seasonal shifts change. You'll also be able to adjust your approach in response to changes in Amazon's commission rates, or to take advantage of new opportunities in your niche.

In short, measuring and analyzing your content's performance is essential for becoming a top-performing Amazon Associates affiliate. Don't neglect this crucial step in your content creation process. By tracking your metrics and making adjustments, you'll be able to continually improve your results and generate more revenue.

Remember, driving targeted traffic to your website takes time and consistent effort. Experiment with different strategies, analyze the results, and refine your approach based on your audience's preferences and behavior. In the next chapter, we will focus on optimizing conversions and maximizing your earnings as an Amazon Associates affiliate marketer.

Chapter 5: Expert Conversion Tips

Are you an Amazon affiliate looking to make more money from your referral links? If so, you're in the right place. This chapter will provide expert tips on how to increase your Amazon affiliate earnings by optimizing conversions. By understanding the best practices for link placement, product promotion, and customer engagement, you can maximize your earnings as an Amazon Associate. Keep reading to learn more about how to increase your Amazon affiliate earnings.

Understand Your Audience

In order to maximize your earnings as an Amazon affiliate, you need to have a deep understanding of your audience. Knowing your audience is critical to selecting the right products, designing your website effectively, and crafting compelling product descriptions. Without understanding your audience, you may struggle to generate the kind of traffic and conversions that you need to earn substantial commissions.

To start, you should think about the demographics of your audience. Who are they? What are their interests, needs, and preferences? What are their pain points, and how can you address them through your product selection and website design? Understanding these details will help you to better tailor your content to meet the needs of your audience and increase conversions.

Beyond demographic data, you should also pay attention to the behavior of your audience.

What pages on your website are they visiting the most? Which products are they clicking on, and which are they buying? What kind of content seems to be most engaging for your audience? Understanding these behavioral patterns will allow you to optimize your website design and content to better meet the needs of your audience.

To gain more insights into your audience, consider running surveys or using analytics tools to track user behavior. The more you can learn about your audience, the more effectively you can design your website, select products, and craft content to drive conversions and maximize your Amazon affiliate earnings.

Choose the Right Products

One of the most important factors in maximizing your Amazon affiliate earnings is selecting the right products to promote on your website. Choosing products that are not a good fit for your audience or that have a low conversion rate can result in a significant decrease in your earnings.

To choose the right products, start by understanding your audience. What are their interests, needs, and preferences? What are their pain points? What solutions are they looking for? Once you have a clear understanding of your audience, you can look for products that align with their needs and interests.

When selecting products, pay attention to their conversion rate. You can use the Amazon Associates dashboard to see the conversion rate for each product. Products with a high conversion rate are more likely to generate earnings for you. However, keep in mind that conversion rate is not the only factor to consider. You also want to promote products that have a good commission rate and are relevant to your audience.

Another factor to consider is product price. Generally, higher-priced products have a higher commission rate. However, you should also consider whether the product is affordable for your audience. If the product is too expensive for your audience, they are unlikely to purchase it, no matter how great the commission rate is.

In addition to the above factors, you should also consider the seasonality of the product. For example, if you are promoting holiday gifts, you will want to choose products that are popular during the holiday season. Similarly, if you are promoting products for summer, you will want to choose products that are relevant to the season.

Choosing the right products is a crucial step in optimizing conversions and maximizing earnings as an Amazon affiliate. By understanding your audience, selecting products with a high conversion rate and good commission rate, and considering factors such as product price and seasonality, you can increase your earnings and grow your affiliate business.

Improve Your Website Design

In the world of online marketing, first impressions are crucial. That's why the design of your website is essential in converting visitors into buyers. When it comes to increasing your Amazon affiliate earnings, your website design plays a significant role. Here are some expert tips on how to improve your website design for better conversion rates.

1. Keep it simple and clutter-free: The design of your website should be clean, simple, and easy to navigate. Avoid cluttering your website with too many graphics, fonts, or images. Instead, focus on creating a website that is user-friendly and visually appealing.

2. Use color psychology: Colors are essential in web design. Certain colors can evoke specific emotions and trigger certain behaviors in visitors. For example, red can create a sense of urgency, while blue can be calming and trustworthy. Choose colors that align with your brand, but also consider their impact on your audience.

3. Optimize your website for mobile: At the present time, more than half of all traffic on the Internet comes from mobile devices. That's why it's crucial to have a website that is optimized for mobile users. Ensure that your website is responsive and adjusts to different screen sizes.

4. Create a strong visual hierarchy: A strong visual hierarchy guides visitors through your website, emphasizing the most critical information. Use larger fonts for headlines, subheadings, and call-to-actions. Ensure that important information is above the fold, so visitors don't have to scroll down to find it.

5. Incorporate social proof: Social proof can increase trust and credibility in your website visitors. Incorporate reviews, testimonials, and user-generated content into your website design. This will help potential buyers feel more confident in their purchase decisions.

By implementing these website design tips, you can improve your website's user experience and increase conversion rates. Remember to keep it simple, use color psychology, optimize for mobile, create a strong visual hierarchy, and incorporate social proof.

Enhance Your Product Descriptions

A description of a product can help it sell or not. When a potential customer visits your website, they want to know everything about the product they're interested in, and they want it in an easy-to-digest format. Your job is to provide them with all the information they need to make a purchasing decision.

Here are some tips for enhancing your product descriptions:

1. Highlight the Features and Benefits

Your customers want to know what the product does and how it can benefit them. Highlight the most important features and explain how they can improve the user's life.

2. Use Persuasive Language

Your product descriptions should use persuasive language that makes your readers feel like they need to buy the product. Use power words and positive language to encourage them to take action.

3. Provide Context

Sometimes a customer needs context to fully understand the benefits of a product. If you're selling a piece of furniture, for example, explain how it can fit in with other furniture items or how it can transform the look of a room.

4. Add High-Quality Images

Images can make a big difference in how customers perceive your product. High-quality images can show off the product's features and give customers a better understanding of how it looks.

5. Be Honest

Your product descriptions should be accurate and honest. Don't exaggerate the features or benefits to make the product sound better than it actually is. If a product has limitations or drawbacks, be honest about them.

By taking the time to create well-crafted product descriptions, you can increase the likelihood of a customer making a purchase. Remember, the goal is to provide customers with all the information they need to make an informed decision. By doing so, you can maximize your earnings as an Amazon affiliate.

Implement Effective Call-to-Actions

Now that you have successfully chosen the right products for your audience and improved your website design and product descriptions, it's time to make sure that your audience knows exactly what actions you want them to take.

This is where an effective call-to-action (CTA) comes into play. A call-to-action is simply a phrase or button that prompts your audience to take action, such as "Buy Now" or "Click Here."

Here are some tips to help you implement effective CTAs:

1. Use Action-Oriented Language: Your CTAs should be short, direct, and actionable. Use phrases that create a sense of urgency or excitement, such as "Limited Time Offer" or "Don't Miss Out."

2. Use Eye-Catching Design: Your CTAs should stand out on your website. Use bold colors, contrasting fonts, or arrows to draw attention to your CTAs.

3. Place CTAs Strategically: Your CTAs should be strategically placed on your website where your audience is most likely to take action. Common placement locations include within your blog post, on your sidebar, or at the bottom of your product pages.

4. Use Multiple CTAs: Don't be afraid to use multiple CTAs on your website. Different CTAs should be used for different products or sections of your website. This helps to ensure that your audience is always aware of the next step they should take.

5. Test and Refine: Like everything else in the world of affiliate marketing, testing and refining is key. Determine which CTAs work best for your audience by testing them out. Refine and adjust your CTAs based on the results you receive.

By implementing effective CTAs, you will be able to guide your audience toward taking action and ultimately increase your Amazon affiliate earnings.

Use Reviews and Testimonials to Boost Credibility

One of the most effective ways to increase conversions and maximize earnings as an Amazon affiliate is by using customer reviews and testimonials. Reviews and testimonials serve as social proof, demonstrating that others have found the product valuable and trustworthy. This can go a long way in building trust with your audience and increasing the likelihood that they will make a purchase through your affiliate link.

So, how can you use reviews and testimonials effectively on your website?

Here are a few tips:

1. Curate Reviews: Take the time to read through customer reviews and choose the ones that best showcase the benefits and features of the product. Highlight the most relevant reviews prominently on your website, making it easy for visitors to see the positive feedback.

2. Use Images: Consider including images of customers who have provided testimonials. This helps to add credibility to the testimonial and can make it feel more personal.

3. Include Negative Reviews: While it may seem counterintuitive, including some negative reviews can actually help to boost credibility. It shows that you are transparent and that you value honesty. Just make sure that the negative reviews you include are balanced with positive reviews and that they don't deter too many potential customers.

4. Create a Dedicated Testimonial Page: Having a dedicated page on your website for customer testimonials can be a powerful way to showcase social proof. This allows visitors to see a variety of feedback in one place and can increase their trust in the product.

By leveraging customer reviews and testimonials, you can boost your credibility as an Amazon affiliate and increase the likelihood that visitors will convert into buyers. Just remember to curate the reviews carefully, use images when possible, include negative reviews in a balanced way, and consider creating a dedicated testimonial page. With these tips in mind, you can enhance your website's social proof and maximize your earnings.

Leverage Social Proof

Social proof refers to the psychological phenomenon where people are more likely to make decisions based on the actions of others. As an Amazon affiliate, you can use social proof to your advantage by showcasing positive reviews and testimonials on your website.

Customers are more likely to purchase a product if they see that other people have already bought and enjoyed it. Therefore, featuring genuine reviews and testimonials can go a long way in increasing your conversions and maximizing your earnings.

Here are some tips to leverage social proof effectively:

1. Feature customer reviews: Add customer reviews to your product pages to provide social proof that your products are worth buying. Make sure to include both positive and negative reviews as this shows that the reviews are genuine.

2. Show product ratings: Display product ratings on your website to give potential buyers a quick glance at the quality of the product. A high rating can also increase trust in your website.

3. Highlight user-generated content: Encourage your audience to share photos and videos of themselves using the products. This will not only create a sense of community around your brand but also show potential buyers that people are already using and enjoying the products.

4. Use influencer endorsements: If you have partnerships with influencers, feature their endorsements on your website. This can create a halo effect around your products, making them seem more desirable.

By leveraging social proof, you can increase the trust and credibility of your website, which in turn can lead to higher conversions and earnings. Remember to always be genuine in your use of social proof and use it to enhance the value of your website to your audience.

Optimize Your Product Links and Banners

When it comes to promoting products as an Amazon Associate, the product links and banners you use are crucial. These links and banners are how you earn commissions, so it's important to optimize them for maximum conversion rates.

Firstly, make sure your links and banners are relevant to the content on your website. If you have a blog post about camping gear, don't link to a random beauty product. This not only looks unprofessional, but it will also confuse your audience and reduce the likelihood of them clicking on the link.

Additionally, choose products with high ratings and positive reviews. These products are more likely to convert as customers will be more likely to trust and purchase products with positive feedback from other customers.

Next, make sure your links and banners are prominently placed on your website. You want to make it as easy as possible for your audience to find and click on these links. You can experiment with different placement locations and track which positions result in the highest conversion rates.

When using banners, make sure they are visually appealing and relevant to the product you are promoting. Use high-quality images and attention-grabbing headlines to capture your audience's attention. You can also add a call-to-action button within the banner to encourage clicks.

Lastly, use text links in addition to banners. Sometimes, a simple text link can be more effective than a flashy banner. Make sure your text links are descriptive and use strong keywords to entice your audience to click on the link.

In summary, optimizing your product links and banners requires relevance, high-quality visuals, prominent placement, and strategic use of text links. By implementing these tips, you can increase the likelihood of your audience clicking on your links and earning more commissions as an Amazon Associate.

Test, Measure, and Optimize for Maximum Conversions

One of the most important steps to take when it comes to increasing your Amazon affiliate earnings is to continually test, measure, and optimize your efforts. You need to be able to track your progress and make adjustments accordingly if you want to see the best results possible.

To get started with testing, make sure that you have a clear understanding of your goals and what you're trying to achieve. Do you want to increase clicks on your product links? Improve your conversion rate? Boost the amount of revenue you earn from each click? Identify your priorities so that you can tailor your testing accordingly.

Once you know what you're trying to achieve, start experimenting with different approaches. Test out different calls-to-action, try using different product images or videos, or experiment with different placement of your links and banners. Try A/B testing to compare the effectiveness of different approaches, and use analytics tools to measure the impact of each change.

As you start to see results, keep track of your progress and analyze the data to identify trends and patterns. This will help you to understand which strategies are working best and where you should focus your efforts. Keep testing and optimizing your efforts, and make adjustments as needed to ensure that you're always getting the best possible results.

In addition to testing and measuring your efforts, be sure to regularly optimize your website and content. Keep your site up-to-date with the latest design trends and features, and continually refine your content to ensure that it's engaging, relevant, and informative.

By continually testing, measuring, and optimizing your efforts, you'll be able to achieve maximum conversions and earnings from your Amazon affiliate program. Remember to keep your audience in mind, choose the right products, enhance your website and product descriptions, implement effective calls-to-action, and leverage social proof. With these tips and a commitment to testing and optimization, you can take your Amazon affiliate earnings to the next level.

By implementing these conversion optimization strategies, you can enhance your affiliate marketing efforts and maximize your earnings as an Amazon Associates affiliate marketer. In the next chapter, we will delve into effective ways to scale your affiliate business and expand your reach for long-term success.

Chapter 6: Scaling Your Affiliate Business with Amazon Associates Program

Are you ready to take your Amazon Associates Program affiliate business to the next level? This chapter of the book provides key insights into how to expand your reach, increase your profits, and maximize your success with the Amazon Associates Program. We will discuss the key strategies presented and provide you with actionable tips on how to scale your affiliate business with the Amazon Associates Program. So, let's get started!

Understanding the Importance of Scaling Your Affiliate Business

When it comes to affiliate marketing, the sky's the limit for potential earnings. However, as with any business, to see continued growth and success, scaling is a necessary step. By expanding your reach and maximizing your earnings potential, you can take your Amazon Associates Program to the next level.

Scaling your affiliate business means expanding your reach beyond your current audience. This can be achieved by utilizing a variety of traffic sources, including social media platforms, blogs, email marketing, and even collaborations with other affiliates and influencers.

In addition to reaching a broader audience, scaling also means diversifying your product promotions and niches. By tapping into a variety of product categories, you can avoid putting all your eggs in one basket and potentially missing out on lucrative opportunities.

Overall, scaling your affiliate business is essential for long-term success in the Amazon Associates Program. It allows you to expand your reach, maximize earnings, and tap into new niches and opportunities. By implementing the strategies outlined in Chapter 6, you can take your affiliate business to new heights and achieve greater success than ever before.

Tips for Expanding Your Reach with the Amazon Associates Program

Expanding your reach with the Amazon Associates Program is a crucial step in scaling your affiliate business. The program provides ample opportunities to reach a wider audience and increase your chances of earning higher commissions. To help you get started, here are some tips:

1. Search Engine Optimization: Search engine optimization (SEO) can help you attract more organic traffic to your website. Use keywords related to your niche and product offerings to optimize your website's content. Make sure your website is user-friendly, mobile-friendly, and has fast loading times.

2. Leverage Social Media: Social media is a powerful tool for reaching a broader audience. Use social media platforms like Facebook, Instagram, and Twitter to promote your affiliate links and product offerings. Encourage your target audience to visit your website by creating engaging content.

3. Join Niche Communities: Niche communities are online platforms where people with similar interests gather to discuss and share information. Join relevant forums, groups, and communities related to your niche. Share your affiliate links, engage with members, and provide valuable insights to build your credibility and authority in the community.

4. Use Paid Advertising: Paid advertising is an effective way to reach a specific audience. You can use Google AdWords, Facebook Ads, and other advertising platforms to target people interested in your niche. Make sure your ad copy and landing page are relevant, engaging, and persuasive.

5. Offer Incentives: Offering incentives to your audience can help boost your affiliate sales. You can offer free ebooks, discounts, or other incentives to people who purchase products through your affiliate links. Make sure the incentives align with your niche and product offerings.

By following these tips, you can expand your reach and maximize your earning potential with the Amazon Associates Program. Remember, building a successful affiliate business takes time and effort. Keep experimenting, analyzing, and optimizing your strategy to achieve long-term success.

The Power of Niche Marketing in Scaling Your Affiliate Business

One of the most effective ways to scale your affiliate business with the Amazon Associates Program is by focusing on niche marketing. This means honing in on a specific market segment and tailoring your content, product promotions, and marketing efforts to appeal to their specific needs and interests.

Niche marketing is a powerful strategy for several reasons. Firstly, it allows you to differentiate yourself from the competition by focusing on a unique angle or sub-topic within your niche. This can help you build a loyal following of engaged readers and customers who appreciate your expertise and insights.

Additionally, by narrowing your focus, you can create more targeted content and promotions that speak directly to your audience's pain points and desires. This can help you boost conversions and maximize your earnings by increasing the relevance and value of your recommendations.

Finally, niche marketing can help you establish yourself as a thought leader or authority within your space. By consistently producing high-quality content and promotions that resonate with your audience, you can build a strong reputation and grow your network of industry connections.

To succeed with niche marketing, it's important to research your target audience thoroughly and understand their needs and preferences. Use tools like Google Trends and social media analytics to identify trending topics and popular keywords within your niche, and stay up-to-date with industry news and developments to keep your content fresh and relevant.

Ultimately, the key to successful niche marketing is to provide value and build trust with your audience. By consistently delivering helpful and informative content, and recommending products that genuinely meet their needs, you can establish a loyal following and drive long-term growth and profitability for your affiliate business.

Maximizing Earnings with Multiple Traffic Sources and Platforms

In today's fast-paced digital world, relying on a single traffic source to drive traffic to your affiliate website is a risky business strategy. This is especially true when it comes to the Amazon Associates Program. Diversifying your traffic sources and platforms can help you reach a wider audience and increase your earnings potential.

One of the most effective ways to diversify your traffic sources is to leverage social media platforms such as Facebook, Instagram, Twitter, and Pinterest. Each platform has its unique audience, and you can use this to your advantage by creating tailored content and promotional strategies that resonate with your followers.

Another effective way to diversify your traffic sources is to explore paid advertising channels such as Google Ads, Facebook Ads, and Amazon Sponsored Products. Paid advertising can help you drive targeted traffic to your affiliate website and generate sales quickly. However, it's important to ensure that your ad campaigns are properly optimized to maximize your ROI.

Aside from diversifying your traffic sources, it's also important to leverage different platforms such as blogs, YouTube, and podcasts to reach a wider audience. For instance, you can create a YouTube channel that features product reviews, tutorials, and how-to guides related to the products you're promoting on Amazon. This can help you build a loyal following and drive traffic to your website through video marketing.

In summary, maximizing your earnings with the Amazon Associates Program requires you to diversify your traffic sources and platforms. By exploring different social media platforms, paid advertising channels, and content formats, you can reach a wider audience and increase your earnings potential. However, it's important to ensure that your promotional strategies are properly optimized and aligned with your target audience's interests and preferences.

Diversifying Your Product Promotions to Boost Affiliate Sales

As an affiliate marketer, you are not limited to promoting just one type of product. In fact, diversifying your product promotions is key to boosting your affiliate sales and maximizing your earning potential with the Amazon Associates Program.

One way to diversify your product promotions is to choose a variety of products that cater to different needs and interests. For example, if you are promoting beauty products, you can promote skincare products for people with dry skin, anti-aging products for older people, and makeup products for people who love to experiment with different looks.

Another way to diversify your product promotions is to explore different categories within Amazon. Amazon has a vast selection of products, including home and kitchen, sports and outdoors, and electronics. By promoting products across different categories, you can reach a wider audience and increase your chances of making more sales.

It's also important to keep up with the latest trends and seasonal products. By promoting products that are popular or in demand during a particular season or trend, you can take advantage of the increased interest and boost your affiliate sales.

In addition, don't be afraid to experiment with different types of promotions, such as deals and discounts, gift guides, and product reviews. Different types of promotions appeal to different audiences and can help you reach a wider range of potential customers.

By diversifying your product promotions, you can increase your affiliate sales and grow your business with the Amazon Associates Program. Keep in mind that it's important to promote products that you believe in and that resonate with your audience to maintain your credibility as an affiliate marketer.

Creating Content That Resonates with Your Target Audience

As an Amazon affiliate, creating high-quality and relevant content is critical to the success of your affiliate business. Your target audience is looking for information, and they will only purchase products from you if they feel you are a reliable source of information.

To create content that resonates with your audience, you need to understand their needs and preferences. Your content should provide valuable insights and recommendations that help your readers make informed purchasing decisions. For instance, if you're promoting a specific product category, provide a list of the best products in that category, or share personal experiences of using the products.

To make your content more engaging, use a variety of formats like blog posts, videos, podcasts, and infographics. Video content is particularly useful for product reviews, tutorials, and demonstrations, while infographics can make complex information easier to understand. Don't forget to include links to relevant products within your content.

In addition, it's essential to create a consistent brand voice across your content. Use a tone and language that resonates with your target audience, and create a personality that aligns with your brand values. Be authentic and honest with your opinions to build trust with your readers.

Lastly, always keep track of your content performance. Use tools like Google Analytics to see which pieces of content are performing best and what channels are driving traffic to your website. Based on this data, refine your content strategy to optimize your content for better results.

Creating content that resonates with your target audience is a key factor in scaling your affiliate business with the Amazon Associates Program. By following these tips, you'll be able to create engaging content that converts your readers into loyal customers.

Developing an Email Marketing Strategy for Long-term Success

Email marketing is an essential component of any successful affiliate business. It's a great way to stay in touch with your audience and provide them with valuable content that they can use to make informed purchasing decisions.

The first step to developing an effective email marketing strategy is to build a targeted email list. This means collecting the email addresses of individuals who have expressed interest in your niche or products.

Once you have a list, it's important to create an email series that provides value to your subscribers. This could be in the form of informative blog posts, helpful product reviews, or exclusive promotions.

One thing to keep in mind is that you should always be looking for ways to provide value to your subscribers. If you only send promotional emails, your subscribers will quickly lose interest and unsubscribe.

Another important aspect of email marketing is to ensure that your emails are mobile-friendly. With more and more people accessing emails on their smartphones, it's important that your emails are easy to read and navigate on smaller screens.

Finally, be sure to track the success of your email campaigns. This includes metrics such as open rates, click-through rates, and conversion rates. By analyzing this data, you can identify what's working and what's not, and make changes to optimize your email marketing strategy for long-term success.

Collaborating with Other Affiliates and Influencers to Grow Your Network

When it comes to scaling your affiliate business, it's crucial to focus on building strong relationships with other affiliates and influencers in your industry. By collaborating with others, you can expand your reach, boost your credibility, and ultimately grow your affiliate network.

One way to get started with collaborating is to join online communities or forums related to your niche. These platforms provide a space for you to connect with other affiliates and influencers who share your interests. You can exchange ideas, share tips and tricks, and even partner up on campaigns or projects.

Another effective approach is to reach out to other affiliates or influencers directly. You can start by offering to promote their products in exchange for them promoting yours. This can be a great way to expand your reach and tap into new audiences that you may not have access to otherwise.

To take your collaboration efforts to the next level, consider hosting joint webinars, podcasts, or live events. By doing so, you can combine your skills and expertise with those of other influencers or affiliates, and offer a unique experience to your audience.

Collaborating with others can also help you stay up-to-date on the latest trends and best practices in your niche. You can learn from other experts and gain insights that can help you refine your own strategy.

Ultimately, building relationships with other affiliates and influencers can be a powerful way to grow your network and scale your affiliate business. Don't be afraid to reach out and make connections – you never know where it may lead.

Tracking Metrics and Analyzing Performance Data to Optimize Your Strategy

Once you have implemented your strategy to scale your affiliate business and expand your reach, it's important to track your progress and analyze performance data to ensure that you're on the right track. The Amazon Associates Program provides you with tools to track your earnings, traffic, and conversions. Here are some key metrics you should be tracking:

1. Click-through rate (CTR): The amount of visitors that you drive to your site through an affiliate link.

2. Conversion rate: The percentage of visitors who complete a purchase after clicking on your affiliate link.

3. Earnings per click (EPC): How much money you make per visitor to your link.

4. Traffic sources: The sources of your traffic, such as search engines, social media, and email campaigns.

5. Products: The products that are generating the most clicks and conversions.

Once you have tracked these metrics, you can analyze them to identify trends and patterns. For example, if you notice that a particular product is generating a high number of clicks but not many conversions, you may need to adjust your promotion strategy or create more targeted content. Or, if you notice that most of your traffic is coming from social media, you may want to focus on expanding your presence on other platforms.

In addition to tracking metrics, it's important to analyze your performance data on a regular basis to optimize your strategy. You can use the insights gained from your data analysis to make informed decisions about where to invest your time and resources.

Scaling your affiliate business requires careful planning, strategic partnerships, and continuous innovation. Regularly assess your progress, set ambitious goals, and adapt your strategies based on market trends and audience feedback. By implementing these scaling techniques, you can take your affiliate business to new heights of success.

In the next chapter, we will discuss essential tips for maintaining and optimizing your affiliate business for long-term profitability.

Chapter 7 Key Strategies for Maintaining Your Amazon Affiliate Business

Are you an Amazon affiliate looking to maintain and grow your business?

We'll be discussing some key strategies that you can use to ensure that your Amazon affiliate business is successful and continues to thrive. From optimizing your website and understanding the right marketing techniques to track your progress and improving customer engagement, we'll cover everything you need to know about maintaining and optimizing your affiliate business. By following the advice in this chapter, you'll be well on your way to running a profitable Amazon affiliate business.

Understanding the Importance of Maintaining Your Amazon Affiliate Business

Building a successful affiliate business with Amazon takes time, effort, and dedication. But once you've achieved success, it's essential to maintain and optimize your business to ensure continued growth and profitability. In this chapter, we'll discuss key strategies for maintaining your Amazon affiliate business.

First and foremost, it's important to understand the significance of maintaining your affiliate business. Without regular upkeep, your business could stagnate and eventually decline. This means less traffic, fewer sales, and less revenue. To avoid this, you must be proactive in managing your business.

One critical aspect of maintaining your Amazon affiliate business is to evaluate its performance regularly. This includes tracking key metrics like traffic, click-through rates, and conversion rates. By regularly analyzing this data, you can identify areas where your business is excelling and where it could improve.

Improving your website design and user experience is also essential for maintaining your business. Visitors are more likely to make purchases on a website that looks professional and is easy to navigate. Focus on creating a clean, user-friendly design that's optimized for both desktop and mobile devices.

Another way to maintain your affiliate business is by creating high-quality content to attract more visitors. This includes product reviews, how-to guides, and informative blog posts that offer value to your audience. The more value you provide, the more likely visitors will be to trust your recommendations and make purchases.

Expanding your niche and diversifying your product offerings can also help maintain your business. By broadening your focus and adding more product categories, you can attract a wider audience and reduce your reliance on any single product or category.

Finally, staying up-to-date with Amazon's policies and guidelines is crucial for maintaining your affiliate business. The program's rules can change, and it's essential to remain compliant to avoid penalties or even losing your affiliate account.

Evaluating Your Affiliate Business Performance Regularly

As an Amazon affiliate, it's important to constantly evaluate the performance of your business. This will help you understand what is working well and what needs improvement, so you can adjust your strategy accordingly and maximize your earning potential. Here are a few key metrics to consider when evaluating your affiliate business performance:

Conversion Rate: Your conversion rate is the percentage of visitors who make a purchase after clicking on your affiliate link. This is a crucial metric because it directly impacts your earnings. A low conversion rate may indicate that your website is not effectively promoting the products or that you're targeting the wrong audience.

Traffic: You want to monitor your website traffic to see how many visitors you're attracting and how they're engaging with your content. Analyze which pages and posts are getting the most traffic, which sources are driving the most traffic (search engines, social media, etc.), and which keywords are bringing in the most traffic.

Revenue: Your revenue is the amount of money you earn through your affiliate links. Keep track of your monthly revenue, as well as which products are generating the most revenue. This will help you identify which products to promote more heavily or which products may need to be replaced with more profitable ones.

Click-Through Rate: Your click-through rate is the percentage of visitors who click on your affiliate links after visiting your website. This metric can give you insights into which links and calls to action are resonating with your audience.

By evaluating your affiliate business performance regularly, you can identify areas for improvement and make data-driven decisions to optimize your earnings. Set aside time each month to review your metrics and adjust your strategy accordingly.

Improving Your Website Design and User Experience

As an Amazon affiliate, your website is the backbone of your business. It is the primary channel through which you can engage with your audience, showcase your products, and drive conversions. Hence, optimizing your website design and user experience (UX) is critical to your affiliate business success.

Here are some key strategies to improve your website design and UX:

1. Keep it Simple: Your website design should be clean, intuitive, and easy to navigate. Avoid cluttered pages, unnecessary graphics, and confusing layouts. Use a simple color scheme, readable fonts, and well-organized content.

2. Make it Mobile-Friendly: With more than 50% of internet users accessing websites on mobile devices, it is essential to ensure that your website is mobile-responsive. Test your website on different devices and platforms to ensure it works smoothly across all.

3. Speed it Up: Your website speed can significantly impact your UX and search engine rankings. Use tools like GTmetrix, Pingdom, or Google PageSpeed Insights to analyze your website's speed and identify any issues. Compress images, reduce redirects, and leverage caching to improve your website speed.

4. Optimize for Search Engines: Your website should be optimized for search engines (SEO) to improve your visibility and organic traffic. Use keyword research to identify relevant search terms, include meta titles and descriptions, optimize your images, and create quality content.

5. Prioritize Your Calls-to-Action: Your calls-to-action (CTAs) should be prominently placed and strategically worded to drive conversions. Use clear language, highlight benefits, and provide urgency to encourage visitors to click on your links.

By improving your website design and UX, you can enhance your visitors' experience, increase engagement, and drive conversions. Regularly review and update your website to ensure it stays relevant, effective, and user-friendly.

Creating High-Quality Content to Attract More Visitors

One of the most effective ways to attract visitors to your Amazon affiliate website is by creating high-quality content that is both engaging and informative. By producing content that is both valuable and relevant to your niche, you can help build a loyal following of visitors who will keep coming back for more.

Below you will find some guidelines to help you produce quality content.

1. Understand Your Target Audience: The first step to creating high-quality content is to understand who your target audience is. How would you describe their interests, needs, and pain points? By understanding your audience, you can tailor your content to their specific needs, which will help make it more appealing and valuable to them.

2. Focus on Quality Over Quantity: When it comes to content creation, quality is always more important than quantity. Rather than trying to produce a large volume of content, focus on creating content that is well-researched, well-written, and visually appealing. This will help you build a reputation as a reliable source of information and help you stand out from your competitors.

3. Use Visuals to Enhance Your Content: Incorporating visuals like images, infographics, and videos can help make your content more engaging and appealing to your audience. Not only do visuals make your content more interesting, but they can also help break up long blocks of text and make it easier to digest.

4. Make Your Content Shareable: To increase the reach of your content, make sure it is easy for visitors to share it on social media platforms like Facebook, Twitter, and LinkedIn. By making your content shareable, you can help extend your reach and attract more visitors to your site.

By focusing on creating high-quality content, you can help attract more visitors to your Amazon affiliate website and build a loyal following of readers who are more likely to make a purchase through your affiliate links.

Expanding Your Niche and Diversifying Your Product Offerings

One of the key strategies for maintaining and optimizing your Amazon affiliate business is expanding your niche and diversifying your product offerings. While it's important to have a focus niche that you're knowledgeable and passionate about, it's also crucial to expand beyond your niche and offer a variety of products that can appeal to a wider audience.

To begin expanding your niche, start by researching related products and categories that your target audience may be interested in.

For example, if you have a website focused on home decor, you can expand your niche by adding products for gardening or kitchen accessories. This can help you reach a wider audience and attract new visitors to your website.

Diversifying your product offerings is also important for long-term success in the Amazon affiliate program. By offering a variety of products, you can reduce your reliance on a single product or category, which can be impacted by market changes or shifts in consumer preferences. This can also help you maximize your earnings potential, as different products may have different commission rates and higher-priced items can lead to higher earnings.

When adding new products to your website, be sure to carefully consider the relevance and quality of the products. Ensure they align with your overall brand and messaging, and provide value to your audience. You should also consider adding product reviews and comparisons to help your visitors make informed purchasing decisions.

Finally, as you expand your niche and diversify your product offerings, don't forget to monitor your performance data to identify which products are performing well and which may need to be reevaluated. Regularly evaluating and adjusting your product offerings can help you stay competitive and relevant in your niche, and ultimately lead to increased earnings in the Amazon affiliate program.

Building a Strong Social Media Presence

In today's digital age, social media has become an essential tool for any business looking to expand its online presence. As an Amazon affiliate, building a strong social media presence is critical to driving traffic to your website and promoting your affiliate products to a wider audience.

There are several key steps you can take to establish a robust social media presence:

1. Choose the right platforms:

There are different types of social media platforms. Each platform has its own strengths and weaknesses, so it's essential to choose the ones that are most suitable for your niche and audience. For example, if your target audience is primarily young adults, Instagram or TikTok might be more effective than Facebook.

2. Create a consistent brand image:

Consistency is key when it comes to branding. Ensure that your social media pages reflect the same branding and messaging as your website to create a cohesive brand image.

3. Engage with your audience:

Social media is all about two-way communication. Engage with your followers by responding to comments and messages promptly. Encourage them to share their opinions and feedback on your products and content.

4. Share high-quality content:

Sharing high-quality, visually appealing content is a great way to attract more followers and increase engagement. Use a mix of images, videos, and text to keep your social media pages fresh and interesting.

5. Use paid advertising:

Paid advertising on social media platforms such as Facebook and Instagram can be an effective way to reach a wider audience. Consider investing in paid ads to promote your affiliate products or drive traffic to your website.

Remember, building a powerful social media presence takes time and hard work. Consistency is key, so make sure you're posting regularly and engaging with your audience consistently. By following these tips, you can establish a robust social media presence that helps to promote your Amazon affiliate business to a wider audience.

Using Data and Analytics to Monitor Your Performance

In order to effectively maintain and optimize your Amazon affiliate business, it's crucial that you utilize data and analytics to monitor your performance. This means taking advantage of the various tools and metrics available to you, such as Google Analytics, Amazon's reporting system, and third-party analytics tools.

By analyzing data such as traffic sources, click-through rates, conversion rates, and earnings, you can identify areas where your affiliate business is excelling and areas that may need improvement. For example, if you notice that a certain product or category is consistently driving higher sales, you may want to focus more on promoting those products or expanding your niche to include similar items.

Similarly, if you're noticing a high bounce rate or low conversion rate on certain pages of your website, you may want to adjust your design or content to better appeal to your audience. By regularly analyzing and adjusting your strategies based on data, you can continuously improve your affiliate business and drive more sales.

It's also important to stay up-to-date on any changes or updates to Amazon's policies and guidelines, as these can directly impact your earnings and performance. By monitoring your data and staying informed on any changes, you can make sure that your affiliate business is always in compliance and optimized for success.

Ultimately, utilizing data and analytics is a crucial component of maintaining and optimizing your Amazon affiliate business. By regularly monitoring your performance and adjusting your strategies accordingly, you can ensure that your business is always on the right track towards success.

Staying Up-to-Date with Amazon's Policies and Guidelines

As an Amazon affiliate, it is crucial to keep yourself updated with the company's policies and guidelines. Amazon regularly updates its terms and conditions, and failure to comply with these rules can result in account suspension or even termination.

To ensure that your affiliate business is safe from any violations, make sure to read and understand Amazon's Operating Agreement thoroughly. This document outlines all the policies and guidelines that affiliates need to follow, including prohibited content, commission structures, and disclosure requirements.

Moreover, Amazon frequently updates its policies, so you need to stay updated with these changes. One way to do this is by subscribing to Amazon's Affiliate Program newsletters and updates. You can also visit Amazon's Associate Central and Seller Central portals to keep yourself updated with the latest changes.

In addition, Amazon provides guidelines for promoting their products. This includes information on using Amazon's logo and trademark, product images, and product descriptions. Failure to comply with these guidelines can result in legal consequences, so it's essential to follow these rules to avoid any issues.

Managing Your Finances and Budgeting for Growth

As an Amazon affiliate, it's essential to manage your finances well to achieve long-term growth and success. This means developing a clear budget and keeping track of all your expenses, from web hosting and domain fees to advertising costs and content creation expenses.

By creating a budget, you can monitor your expenses and revenue streams more closely, which will help you determine where to focus your resources and which areas need more attention. Additionally, keeping track of your finances will also help you better understand your profitability, making it easier to invest in your business and plan for future growth.

One important tip for managing your finances as an Amazon affiliate is to avoid overspending on advertising and other costs. While paid marketing campaigns and other expenses can help grow your business, it's important to prioritize cost-effectiveness and focus on strategies that generate a positive return on investment (ROI). By focusing on ROI, you can minimize your costs and maximize your revenue, allowing you to build a more sustainable and profitable business in the long run.

Another key aspect of financial management for Amazon affiliates is diversification. While it's important to focus on a specific niche or product offering, it's equally important to expand your offerings and diversify your revenue streams. This can include exploring new product categories, developing partnerships with complementary brands, or even launching your own products or services. By diversifying your revenue streams, you can reduce your reliance on any one product or niche and increase your overall revenue potential.

Overall, managing your finances and budgeting for growth is a critical part of building a successful Amazon affiliate business. By creating a clear budget, monitoring your expenses and revenue, and diversifying your revenue streams, you can build a more sustainable, profitable, and successful affiliate business over time.

Investing in Continuous Learning and Professional Development

As an Amazon affiliate marketer, you must understand the importance of staying ahead of the curve when it comes to industry trends, techniques, and tools. Continuously learning and improving your skills and knowledge will help you remain competitive, adaptable, and successful in your affiliate business.

One way to invest in your professional development is to attend industry conferences and events. These events provide valuable opportunities to learn from industry experts, network with other affiliate marketers, and stay updated on the latest trends and technologies.

Another way to invest in your learning is to join relevant online communities, such as forums, Facebook groups, or Slack channels. These communities offer a wealth of information, support, and collaboration opportunities, allowing you to learn from other successful affiliates, ask questions, and share your own knowledge.

Additionally, consider enrolling in online courses or training programs that teach specific skills or strategies related to affiliate marketing. Many platforms offer courses on topics like SEO, social media marketing, email marketing, or content creation that can help you refine your skills and improve your results.

Finally, it's crucial to continuously read blogs, eBooks, and industry publications to stay up-to-date with the latest trends and news related to your niche. Following experts and influencers on social media platforms can also provide valuable insights and tips.

By investing in your continuous learning and professional development, you'll be better equipped to overcome challenges, seize opportunities, and succeed in the competitive world of affiliate marketing. So, make sure to set aside time and budget for learning, training, and improving your skills regularly.

Chapter 8: Conclusion

Congratulations on completing this book! Throughout the chapters, we have explored the blueprint for building a lucrative online business with affiliate marketing through the Amazon Associates program. Now, let's summarize the key points and offer final insights.

Affiliate marketing offers a tremendous opportunity to create a sustainable and profitable online business in today's digital landscape. We have learned that understanding the fundamentals of affiliate marketing is crucial, from how affiliate programs work to the benefits they offer. By choosing a profitable niche aligned with your interests and market demand, you set the foundation for success.

A conversion-focused website is essential for driving traffic and optimizing conversions. Through effective content creation, SEO strategies, and the strategic placement of affiliate links, you can attract organic traffic and increase your earnings potential. Remember, the key is to provide value to your audience through high-quality content that addresses their needs and interests.

Scaling your affiliate business is an exciting phase that allows you to diversify your product portfolio, collaborate with influencers and brands, and expand your reach into international markets. By continually updating and optimizing your content, monitoring affiliate links, and staying informed about industry trends, you can maintain the competitiveness and profitability of your business.

Building a successful online business with affiliate marketing requires dedication, persistence, and adaptability. It is a journey of continuous learning and refinement. Embrace new technologies, leverage data analysis to drive informed decisions, and always prioritize providing value to your audience.

Remember that success is not guaranteed overnight. Patience, effort, and time are required. Stay committed to your goals, be open to experimentation, and don't be afraid to adapt your strategies along the way. Affiliate marketing offers an abundance of opportunities, and with the knowledge and insights gained from this book, you are well-equipped to embark on your own journey toward success.

Keep in mind that the affiliate marketing landscape is ever-evolving. Stay updated with the latest industry trends, changes in regulations, and emerging marketing strategies. Networking with other affiliate marketers, attending industry conferences, and continuous self-education will help you stay ahead of the curve.

As we conclude this book, remember that your success lies in your hands. Believe in yourself, stay focused, and persevere even during challenging times. With determination, creativity, and the right strategies, you can turn your affiliate marketing business into a lucrative venture that offers financial freedom and the opportunity to live life on your terms.

Thank you for joining us on this journey. We wish you the best of luck in creating your own lucrative affiliate marketing business. Remember, the path to success begins with taking the first step and never giving up.

Don't miss out!

Visit the website below and you can sign up to receive emails whenever Chase Richardson publishes a new book. There's no charge and no obligation.

https://books2read.com/r/B-A-DOCZ-AAUKC

BOOKS 2 READ

Connecting independent readers to independent writers.

9 798223 350620